The King's Magician

Sheila Lane and Marion Kemp

CAMBRIDGE UNIVERSITY PRESS
Cambridge
London   New York   New Rochelle
Melbourne   Sydney

The King's Magician

This story is about a country where all the work is carried out by magic. When the King's magician runs away, a new one has to be found quickly. The job is advertised and three applicants compete for the post.

The townspeople and courtiers settle down to watch the first play which is the story of the first applicant, Thomas the Tinker. Thomas says that he can make wishes come true. Next comes the story of Clever Jack, who boasts that he can outwit everyone. Last of all, a little old man shows what he can do, and everyone enjoys his story of Klug and the golden goose, in which a sad princess is made happy.

The King asks his people to choose the new magician by voting for the one they want. When it is seen that the little old man can bring RICHES as well as laughter, he is chosen.

The townspeople and courtiers who watch the plays are the **Playwatchers**. The characters who act in the three stories are the **Playmakers**.

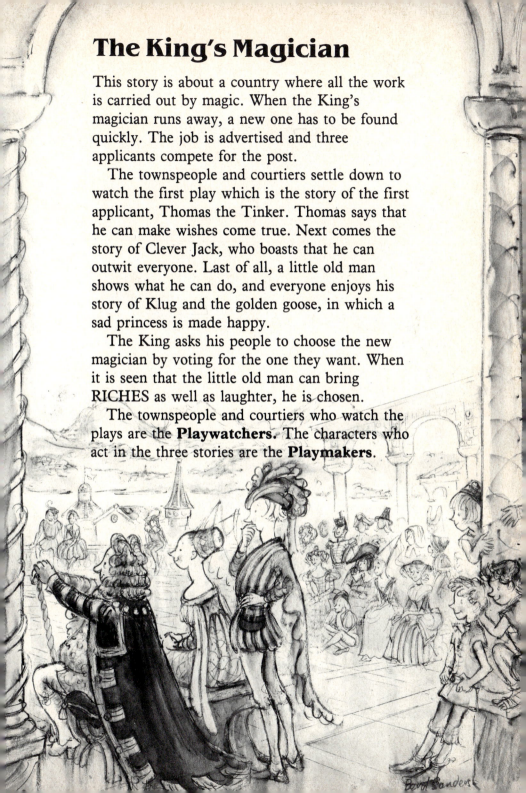

Contents

PLAYWATCHERS

BESSIE BAGGOT ⎤
BERTHA ⎬ women of the town
BELL ⎦

Other people of the town

TOM BONE ⎤
DICK ⎬ workmen
HARRY ⎦

Other workmen

TOWN CRIER
LORD CHAMBERLAIN
HERALD
KING

People of the Court

THOMAS THE TINKER (for first play)
CLEVER JACK (for second play)
THE LITTLE OLD MAN (for third play)

Enter TOWN CRIER, *followed by a group of excited* TOWNSPEOPLE.

TOWN CRIER (*ringing bell*)
O-YEZ! O-YEZ! O-YEZ!
All come to this place
At twelve o' the clock.
O-YEZ! O-YEZ! O-YEZ! (*He goes out.*)

TOWNSPEOPLE What's it all about? What's it all about?

BESSIE I should think it's about the state of this country!
This country's a disgrace! It's an absolute
disgrace!

TOWNSPEOPLE	It's a disgrace! It's a disgrace!
BERTHA	You're right, Bessie.
BELL	Bessie's always right!
BESSIE	And as for getting anything done! Look! (*pointing*) There's rubbish everywhere. It's time we complained to the King.
BERTHA	You do it, Bessie.
BELL	Go on, Bessie! You do it!
BESSIE	All right! We'll make a list of our complaints and then I'll go and tell the King.
TOWNSPEOPLE	Good old Bessie! Good old Bessie!
	(*Enter* TOWN CRIER, *followed by a group of* WORKMEN.)
TOWN CRIER	(*ringing bell*) O-YEZ! O-YEZ! O-YEZ! All come to this place At twelve o' the clock . . . To hear the proclamation Of his majesty, the King. O-YEZ! O-YEZ! O-YEZ! (*He goes out.*)
BESSIE	That's a bit of luck! The King is coming here! Now let's decide about our complaints.
TOM	What's the matter with these women?
DICK	They're complaining about something as usual.

BESSIE Yes, we're making a list of complaints about the state of this country.

BERTHA And we're giving it to the King.

BELL At twelve o'clock today.

TOM It's nothing to do with us. We don't work any more.

BESSIE Humph! We know that!

DICK We're not supposed to work now that Wulfric does everything.

HARRY Wulfric's a magician. He does the work by magic. What's the good of having a magician if we do the work ourselves?

BESSIE But he hasn't been doing the work. No-one's been doing it.

TOWNSPEOPLE No-one's been doing it.

BERTHA No-one's been to mend my tap.

BELL No-one's been to mend my door.

TOM Wulfric does all the work.

TOWNSPEOPLE Oh no, he doesn't!

HARRY Well, we don't know how to work any more. Since Wulfric came and did it all, BY MAGIC, we've forgotten how to work.

(*Enter* TOWN CRIER, *followed by* LORD CHAMBERLAIN *and* COURTIERS.)

TOWN CRIER	(*ringing bell*) O-YEZ! O-YEZ! O-YEZ!
BESSIE	Just a minute! (*putting hand on bell*) Where's the King?
TOWN CRIER	(*to Bessie*) Take your hand off my bell.
CHAMBERLAIN	How dare you put your common hand on the royal bell? What's your name woman?
BESSIE	Bessie Baggot! And I want to see the King.
CHAMBERLAIN	Oh! You can see him all right. The King is coming here at twelve o'clock.
BESSIE	We know that! And when he comes, I've got something to say to him.
CHAMBERLAIN	SAY! People like you don't speak to the King.
BESSIE	We'll see about that! (*The palace clock starts to strike.*)
ALL	(*taking up counting*) ... SIX ... SEVEN ... EIGHT ... NINE ... TEN ... ELEVEN ... TWELVE!

(*Enter* HERALD.)

TOWN CRIER	(*ringing bell*) O-YEZ! O-YEZ! O-YEZ!

(*Enter* KING.)

HERALD	His majesty, the King!
TOWNSPEOPLE	(*pushing Bessie forward*) Go on, Bessie! Go on!
HERALD	Silence for his majesty, the King.
TOWNSPEOPLE	Go on, Bessie!
BESSIE	Not yet! Let's hear what he has to say first.
CHAMBERLAIN	You people must keep quiet, do you understand? You must . . .
KING	Stop fussing, Lord Chamberlain! Just read the proclamation.
CHAMBERLAIN	Oh dear! Now let me see! (*reads*) THIS IS THE PRO . . .CLA. . .MMM. . .
KING	(*impatiently*) PROCLAMATION! I've just said that word. Where are your spectacles? Who can lend the Lord Chamberlain some spectacles?
VARIOUS TOWNSPEOPLE	I can! Take these! Here! Have mine!
CHAMBERLAIN	(*in horror*) I can't use other people's spectacles! They would damage my eyes.
KING	Stop fussing, Lord Chamberlain! I'll just tell everyone the news myself. (*to crowd*) Listen everyone! We're in trouble!
TOWNSPEOPLE	Hear! Hear!

BESSIE	This country's in trouble, all right. It's a disgrace and we've got a lot of complaints.
KING	Who is this woman?
CHAMBERLAIN	A trouble-maker, called Bessie Baggot! If you ask me . . .
BESSIE	Nobody's asking you . . .
KING	Well . . . not yet, anyway! We're in trouble because our royal magician has DISAPPEARED.
TOWNSPEOPLE	Disappeared!
KING	Wulfric has skipped . . . scarpered . . . skidaddled! So now we're in a fix because there's no-one to do the work. (*pointing to workmen*) They're no good! They're useless!
TOWNSPEOPLE	Hear, hear!
KING	I've advertised for a new magician and there are three applicants for the job. (TOWNSPEOPLE *clap*.)
	. . . So I've decided to be a really good, MODERN king . . . and let you do the choosing.
TOWNSPEOPLE	US! DO THE CHOOSING! (TOWNSPEOPLE *clap*.)
KING	(*holding up hand*) Don't get excited! Choosing isn't easy! In fact it will be a great responsibility.
CHAMBERLAIN	It will be a great trouble, if you ask me.
BESSIE	Nobody's asking YOU! The King is asking US.

KING   Yes! But not *all* of you. I'll pick just SIX to be the voters. (*turning to Court*) I'll have you, Lord Chamberlain . . . and you (*pointing*) and YOU. (*turning to townspeople*) I'd better have you, Bessie Baggot . . . and you (*pointing*) . . . and you.

CHAMBERLAIN   Do we . . . er . . . educated people get two votes each?

KING   Certainly not! I'm a modern king. I believe in ONE MAN ONE VOTE. Herald!

HERALD   Yes, your majesty!

KING   Bring in the first applicant.

(HERALD *goes out.*)

Now, get yourselves sorted out . . . Voters over here . . . and watchers over there.

(*Voters make two groups, but Lord Chamberlain makes big gap between his group and Bessie's.*)

(*Enter* HERALD *with* THOMAS THE TINKER.)

HERALD   Bow to the King, Thomas! Bow to the King!

KING   Good gracious! You don't look capable of being a Court magician! How old are you?

THOMAS   Oh! Very old, your majesty!

KING   This isn't a part-time job you know.

THOMAS	Well, it's part-time money!
	(TOWNSPEOPLE *laugh and clap*.)
KING	That will do! We don't want a Court jester! We want a Court magician! What makes you think you can help us, anyway?
THOMAS	An old man like me knows a lot . . . You can see I'm an old tinker man and I've travelled the country picking up all kinds of information. I know about SPELLS . . . CHARMS . . . GOOD LUCK . . .
KING	Well . . . We could do with some GOOD LUCK.
THOMAS	I can . . . MAKE WISHES COME TRUE.
TOWNSPEOPLE	WISHES! HOW? HOW?
THOMAS	The way I made little Rosaleen's wish come true. She was just an ordinary girl who lived only a step from where I live now with my poor old wife.
KING	Very well, Thomas. Show us how to make wishes come true.
THOMAS	(*calls*) Asling! Brian! Rosaleen! (*He goes out*.)
	(*Playwatchers move to side*.)

Here begins the story of The Wishing Stone.

The Wishing Stone

Playmakers

THOMAS THE TINKER

ASLING
BRIAN – her brother
ROSALEEN – her sister

FIRST SPIRIT
SECOND SPIRIT   the spirits of the Wishing Stone
THIRD SPIRIT

FIRST BOGLE
SECOND BOGLE   the food spirits
THIRD BOGLE

FIRST FAIRY
SECOND FAIRY   the dream fairies
THIRD FAIRY

PRINCE CONAL

PRINCESS ORLA
PRINCESS EVA

COOK
POTS   kitchen boys
PANS
FINNIGAN – a page
Other kitchen boys

The Wishing Stone

The Wishing Stone Grove is carried in and hidden by a screen.
ASLING *and* BRIAN *enter. Asling is looking into a hand mirror
and Brian is eating from a pie-dish.*

ASLING   Mirror! Mirror in my hand!
Who is the fairest in the land?

BRIAN   (*between mouthfuls*) I'm sure I've heard those
words before, Asling.

ASLING   I'm glad you've got something in your head,
brother! I thought you were only interested in
something in your stomach.

BRIAN   Well . . . I am more interested in . . . my stomach
. . . than my head . . . but you are only interested
in . . . the OUTSIDE of your head, Asling.

ASLING   Ah! Just look at my beautiful hair! Just look at
my beautiful face! I think I'll put some pink
powder on it today . . . (*calls*) ROSALEEN!
Where is that sister of ours . . .? ROSALEEN!
(*calls louder*) ROSALEEEEEN!

(*Enter* ROSALEEN *with broom.*)

ROSALEEN   Yes, sister?

ASLING   Bring me my box of pink powder. (ROSALEEN *goes
out.*) ROSALEEN! (*Enter* ROSALEEN.) And don't
forget the powder puff.

ROSALEEN   Yes sister. (*She goes out.*)

BRIAN   (*calls*) ROSALEEEEEN! (*Enter* ROSALEEN.)

ROSALEEN   Yes, Brian. What is it?

BRIAN   Bring me the cheesecake from the pantry.

ROSALEEN   But, brother . . .

BRIAN   I don't want BUTS! I want the cheesecake! Fetch
it!

ROSALEEN   But . . . I wanted . . .

15

ASLING You greedy girl! I do believe you wanted that cheesecake for yourself.

ROSALEEN No, no! I never want things for myself.

BRIAN Then what do you want my cheesecake for?

ROSALEEN I wanted to go and take a little bit to poor Anna, the tinker's wife.

BRIAN So now we know where our cheesecakes have been going. You've been giving them away. You bad girl! (*slapping Rosaleen*) You bad girl!

(*Someone is heard knocking on the door.*)

ASLING Don't just stand there, Rosaleen. Go and see who it is.

(ROSALEEN *goes out.*)

BRIAN She's a greedy, good-for-nothing girl!

(*Enter* ROSALEEN *with* THOMAS THE TINKER.)

ROSALEEN It's Thomas, the Tinker.

THOMAS And the top o' the morning to you three dear people! I've come here to thank you for all your kindness to my poor, sick wife. She loved that cheesecake, Rosaleen.

ROSALEEN (*to Thomas*) Ssh! Ssh!

THOMAS Perhaps I'd better start by thanking you, Asling.

ASLING Me!

THOMAS To be sure, Asling, it makes my poor Anna's heart sing for joy every time she sees your beautiful self walk by her window.

ASLING Of course, I am very beautiful. (*looking in mirror*) Mirror! Mirror in my hand! I am the fairest in the land. But . . . I just wish that I had beautiful clothes to go with my beautiful looks.

BRIAN Well! No-one could call me beautiful!

THOMAS To be sure Brian, you're a fine, big fellow. When my poor Anna sees you go by her window, she calls out, 'There goes a fine, strong man.'

BRIAN	I should be even stronger if I could get more to eat. I believe I could eat a whole mountain of food. I wish someone would give me a FOOD MOUNTAIN.
THOMAS	That's a fine wish to be sure. But what about our little Rosaleen? What do you wish for, Rosaleen?
ROSALEEN	Me? Oh, I just want to be happy.
THOMAS	Why, so you will be, my dear. Thomas the Tinker can see your fortune in your face.
ASLING	In her face! There's nothing special about Rosaleen's face. But . . . I've just remembered something . . . You tinkers can tell fortunes. Can you tell my fortune, Thomas?
THOMAS	I can do better than that. I can tell you how to find your fortune for YOURSELF.
ASLING	Tell me where I can find a rich husband who will buy me fine clothes, Thomas.
THOMAS	To be sure, Asling, you should get the rich clothes first and then you'll be able to get a fine husband for yourself afterwards.
BRIAN	Tell me how to find someone who will give me a FOOD MOUNTAIN, Thomas.
THOMAS	To be sure I will! You know Bluebell Bank at the edge of the wood.
ALL THREE	Yes.
THOMAS	If you climb over the bank, you will see a little path running over a field of clover. Climb the stone wall on the far side and you will see a circle of trees in the distance.
ASLING	But I don't want to walk far, Thomas.
BRIAN	I don't want to walk at all.
THOMAS	Those who seek good fortune have to put themselves out a little! As I was saying . . . you will see a circle of trees . . . Walk through the trees and you will be there.
ALL THREE	Where?

THOMAS	In the Wishing Stone Grove. It's a lovely, secret place. You'll see it . . . in the grove.
ALL THREE	See what?
THOMAS	The Wishing Stone. Anyone who sits on the Wishing Stone can wish three times . . . THREE TIMES, mind, and in that way they can get the three things which their hearts most desire.
ALL THREE	Three things!
ASLING	I shall go first. In fact, I shall go now. Goodbye! (*She goes out.*)
BRIAN	Wait for me, Asling. I'm coming too. (*He goes out.*)
ROSALEEN	Do you think the Wishing Stone will keep one wish for me, Thomas? I only want one wish, you know.
THOMAS	You'll get one, my dear. Off you go!

(ROSALEEN *goes out. The screen is removed from in front of the grove and stone.*)

(*to the Playwatchers*) As you can imagine, the beautiful Asling arrived at the Wishing Grove long before that lazy brother of hers. (*He moves aside.*)

(*Enter* ASLING.)

ASLING	Oh dear! How hot and tired I am. I'll rest on this old stone. (*She sits down.*) I wish I had a drink of water to refresh myself.

(*Enter* FIRST SPIRIT *with water.*)

FIRST SPIRIT	Your wish is granted, Beautiful One!
ASLING	Water! So fresh and cool! Thank you! Did I hear you call me Beautiful One?
FIRST SPIRIT	You did, Beautiful One.
ASLING	That's what everyone says. At home, I often look in my mirror and talk to myself.
FIRST SPIRIT	What do you say, Beautiful One?

18

ASLING	I say, 'Mirror! Mirror in my hand! Who is the fairest in the land?' Oh, I wish I had a silver mirror so that I could look at myself.
	(*Enter* SECOND SPIRIT *with a silver mirror.*)
SECOND SPIRIT	Your wish is granted, Beautiful One.
ASLING	A silver mirror! Can I keep it?
SECOND SPIRIT	You can, Beautiful One.
ASLING	This is a much better mirror than the one I have at home. I can see my face . . . my hair . . . but ugh! What a plain dress. I wish I had a beautiful cloak to cover it up.
	(*Enter* THIRD SPIRIT *with cloak.*)
THIRD SPIRIT	Your wish is granted, Beautiful One.
ASLING	Oh, how lovely! Put it round my shoulders. Does it suit me?
THIRD SPIRIT	It does, Beautiful One.
ASLING	(*getting up*) Now I will look for the magic Wishing Stone. Do you know where it is?
ALL SPIRITS	(*pointing*) There, Beautiful One.
ASLING	What? This plain, old stone. Do you mean that I've been sitting on it all the time?
ALL SPIRITS	We do, Beautiful One.
ASLING	Well, that's a relief. I won't have to go any farther. Now for my three wishes. First . . .
FIRST SPIRIT	Your first wish was for cool, fresh water.
SECOND SPIRIT	Your second wish was for a silver mirror.
THIRD SPIRIT	Your third wish was for a beautiful cloak.
ALL SPIRITS	Your three wishes have been granted. (*They go out.*)
ASLING	GRANTED! But I wanted dresses and silk stockings and high heeled shoes and . . . (*angrily*) Where are those creatures? Come back and give me some more wishes. COME BACK . . .! Oh well, I'll have to go and find them for myself. (*She goes out.*)

(Enter BRIAN *from other side. He sits on the stone.)*

BRIAN What a long way! I'm starving. I wish I had something to eat ... anything ... just a crust of bread.

(Enter FIRST BOGLE *with a crust of bread.)*

FIRST BOGLE Your wish is granted, Hungry One.

BRIAN Well, I don't want that. You don't expect me to eat dry bread, do you?

FIRST BOGLE You asked for bread, Hungry One.

BRIAN Did I? Well, I suppose I could eat it. At least I could if I had ...

FIRST BOGLE If you had what, Hungry One?

BRIAN If I had some butter to put on it. I wish I had a bit of butter, then I could eat it.

(Enter SECOND BOGLE *with a small piece of butter.)*

SECOND BOGLE Your wish is granted, Hungry One.

BRIAN Is that all you've brought?

SECOND BOGLE You asked for a bit of butter, Hungry One.

BRIAN Well, I suppose it's better than nothing. I wish I had ...

SECOND BOGLE You wish you had what, Hungry One?

BRIAN Some cheese. I wish I had a piece of cheese to put on the bread and butter.

(Enter THIRD BOGLE *with a piece of cheese.)*

THIRD BOGLE Your wish is granted, Hungry One.

BRIAN I didn't mean a little piece like that. I meant a huge, enormous piece.

THIRD BOGLE Some people think they are lucky to be given anything at all, Hungry One.

BRIAN Well, I want MOUNTAINS OF FOOD. That's what I've come all this way for. *(looking round)* Where's the Wishing Stone. Do you know?

ALL BOGLES *(pointing)* There, Hungry One!

BRIAN	What! This hard old stone! Do you mean I've been sitting on it all the time?
ALL BOGLES	We do.
BRIAN	That's good. I won't have to go any farther. Now for my three wishes. First . . .
FIRST BOGLE	Your first wish was for a crust of bread.
SECOND BOGLE	Your second wish was for a bit of butter.
THIRD BOGLE	Your third wish was for a piece of cheese.
ALL BOGLES	Your three wishes have been granted. (*They go out.*)
BRIAN	GRANTED! But I want MOUNTAINS of food. I want huge breakfasts, enormous dinners and gigantic suppers. (*angrily*) Where are those creatures? Come back and give me some more wishes. COME BACK! I'm going after them. (*He goes out.*)
	(*Enter* ROSALEEN *from other side.*)
ROSALEEN	Oh! What a lovely place! I think I'll sit on this stone and have a rest . . . I'm so very . . . very . . . tired. (*She sleeps.*)
	(FIRST FAIRY *peeps in.*)
FIRST FAIRY	She hasn't asked for anything yet.
	(*Enter* SECOND *and* THIRD FAIRIES, *carrying a piece of net.*)
SECOND FAIRY	She will! She will! (*They cover Rosaleen with net.*)
THIRD FAIRY	Listen! She's talking in her dreams.
ROSALEEN	I wish . . .
ALL FAIRIES	(*bending over Rosaleen*) What do you wish?
ROSALEEN	How I wish I could rest awhile in this secret place and . . . and . . .
ALL FAIRIES	And . . .?
ROSALEEN	And when I wake up, I should see a handsome prince who would carry me far, far away . . . far, far away . . .
ALL FAIRIES	Your wish shall be granted. (*They go out.*)

21

THOMAS	(*to the Playwatchers*) And so it was that the little Rosaleen slept peacefully in the Wishing Grove, dreaming of a handsome prince who would carry her far, far away. Ah! . . . We're in luck! (*Enter* PRINCE CONAL.) The top o' the morning to you, fine sir.
PRINCE CONAL	And the top of the morning to you, old man. Tell me, do you know the way to the King's palace? I'm on my way to choose one of his daughters to be my wife.
THOMAS	If it's a wife you're looking for, you don't need to go looking in palaces. I've got a lovely girl for you, right here. Look! (*He pulls back the net from Rosaleen's face.*)
PRINCE CONAL	(*shrugging*) She's fair enough, but she won't do for me.
THOMAS	And why's that?
PRINCE CONAL	Because I'm Prince Conal of the Royal Blood and I must have a real princess to be my wife.
THOMAS	(*covering Rosaleen*) Ah well! But are you too proud to take a thimbleful of advice from an old tinker?
PRINCE CONAL	I need all the advice I can get. Choosing a bride is a very tricky business.
THOMAS	Choose one who will last! Listen! When you get to the palace, DON'T KNOCK AT THE FRONT DOOR.
PRINCE CONAL	What shall I do then?
THOMAS	Put on some old clothes and go to the back door. Get a job with the cook in the palace kitchen. That way you'll find out about the two princesses and then you'll know which one to choose.
PRINCE CONAL	Well, I can't marry them both. Yes . . . I think that's a very good idea.
THOMAS	(*to the Playwatchers*) The prince hardly looked at Rosaleen. But . . . he'll be back . . . you'll see. I'll just sit here for a while. (*He moves to the side of the arena.*)

(*Enter* KITCHEN BOYS *who put a screen round the Wishing Stone Grove. They are followed by the* COOK, *and* POTS *and* PANS, *carrying kitchen utensils.*)

COOK What a muddle! What a mess!

POTS Where shall I put the pots, cook? (*He puts them on the floor.*)

COOK Not on the floor, you stupid boy! Now you'll have to wash them again. And look at those pans!

PANS What's the matter with them, cook?

COOK They need shining up. Shine them until you can see your stupid faces in them! (*He goes out.*)

POTS Rub the pans, go up and down . . .

PANS Then cook's face will lose its frown! (*Both laugh.*)

(*Enter* FINNIGAN.)

FINNIGAN Cook! Cook! Where's cook?

COOK (*coming in*) I'm coming! I'm coming! I hope you haven't brought any orders from those two princesses, Master Finnigan. I haven't time to attend to their fads and fancies today.

FINNIGAN Don't worry! I've brought you another kitchen boy.

COOK Then you're a good friend to me, Master Finnigan. Bring him in!

FINNIGAN (*calls*) Boy! Conal!

(*Enter* PRINCE CONAL *dressed as a kitchen boy.*)

COOK What do you know about kitchen work, boy?

PRINCE CONAL Nothing yet, cook, but I can learn.

COOK That will be a change. These two (*pointing to Pots and Pans*) can't learn anything.

(*Screams from off stage.*)

PRINCE CONAL What's that terrible noise?

POTS Orla and Eva, two bad-tempered girls.

PANS With beautiful faces and beautiful curls! (*Both laugh.*)

COOK	I'll box your ears! How dare you talk about the princesses like that!
	(*Enter* PRINCESS ORLA *and* PRINCESS EVA *carrying a plate of cakes.*)
PRINCESS ORLA	So THERE you are, Finnigan!
FINNIGAN	ME! Oh no! I'm not here, your highness! (*He runs and hides behind the cook.*)
PRINCESS EVA	Cook! Who sent these cakes upstairs?
COOK	Don't ask me! I'm much too busy to send cakes anywhere.
PRINCESS ORLA	Someone brought them upstairs and they're stale. They're yesterday's stale rock cakes.
PRINCESS EVA	Cakes can't walk upstairs! Someone brought them.
PRINCESS ORLA	It must have been one of those boys. Come here, Pots. (*taking him by the ear*)
PRINCESS EVA	Come here, Pans! (*taking him by the ear*) Now which of you brought these cakes upstairs?
POTS	(*pointing to Pans*) HE DID! (*Both get away.*)
PANS	(*pointing to Pots*)
PRINCESS ORLA	Then you can have them back. Take that one! (*throwing cake at Pots*)
PRINCESS EVA	And you can have that! (*throwing cake at Pans*)
PRINCE CONAL	Don't do that, princesses!
PRINCESS ORLA	And who are you?
PRINCE CONAL	I'm Conal, the new kitchen boy . . . and I didn't bring the cakes because I've only just come!
PRINCESS EVA	(*smiling*) So you're a new boy are you, Conal? Would you like a cake?
PRINCE CONAL	Yes, please!
PRINCESS ORLA	Would you like two cakes, Conal?
PRINCE CONAL	Er . . . well . . . yes please!
PRINCESSES	You GREEDY boy! Take that! And that! (*They pelt Conal with cakes, then go out.*)
POTS	(*laughing*) Orla and Eva, two bad-tempered girls.

24

PANS   (*laughing*) With . . .

COOK   I'll box your ears if you don't get on with your work! Take those pots and pans away.

(POTS *and* PANS *go out with utensils, still laughing.*)

FINNIGAN   Poor Conal! (*wiping Conal's face*) My! What a fine skin you have! It's more like a prince's skin than a kitchen boy's . . .

PRINCE CONAL   (*hurriedly*) Excuse me! I've seen enough! (*He goes out.*)

COOK   He won't last long!

FINNIGAN   Then I'd better give you a hand myself!

(COOK *and* FINNIGAN *go out. The screen is removed from in front of the Wishing Stone Grove.*)

THOMAS   (*to the Playwatchers, as he moves forward*) I'm still here . . . with the little Rosaleen. I wonder how the Prince got on at the palace . . . Do you know, I shouldn't be surprised if . . . Ah yes! Here he comes!

(*Enter* PRINCE CONAL *dressed as a prince again.*)

The top o' the afternoon to you, Prince Conal.

PRINCE CONAL   What a day! I never want to see princesses like those two again as long as I live.

THOMAS   So you're not going to choose one of them to be your wife after all?

PRINCE CONAL   Wife! I should think not!

THOMAS   They say the King's daughters are very beautiful.

PRINCE CONAL   And very bad tempered! Do you know, Thomas, you gave me a good thimbleful of advice when you told me to get a job in the palace kitchen.

THOMAS   Are you ready to listen to me again, prince?

PRINCE CONAL   I am.

THOMAS   (*taking mirror from pocket*) Always choose a bride who will last! If you look in the mirror of Days to Come and say the name of the first princess, you will see her as she will look in twenty years' time.

25

PRINCE CONAL	(*taking mirror*) Orla! Orla! Ugh! She's horrible! I suppose bad temper made her look like that.
THOMAS	Now say the name of the second princess.
PRINCE CONAL	Eva! Eva! Ugh! Even worse!
THOMAS	Now whisper into the glass and say, 'Rosaleen'.
PRINCE CONAL	(*whispering*) Rosaleen! Rosaleen! Ah! What a lovely, happy face. Who is she, Thomas?
THOMAS	Come over here and find out for yourself. (*He takes Prince Conal to the sleeping Rosaleen.*) Say that name again, Conal, but this time a little louder. (*He pulls back the net.*)
PRINCE CONAL	Rosaleen! Rosaleen!
ROSALEEN	(*opening her eyes*) Who called my name? Oh!
PRINCE CONAL	What a lovely smile! What is your name?
ROSALEEN	You said my name. Did you call me?
PRINCE CONAL	I said . . . Rosaleen! Was it your face I saw in the Mirror of Days to Come, dear Rosaleen?
ROSALEEN	What do you mean?
THOMAS	I can tell you what it means. Look into the mirror yourself, Rosaleen, and say, 'Conal! Conal!'
ROSALEEN	(*taking mirror*) Conal! Conal! Oh! What a good, kind face!
PRINCE CONAL	Tell her that it is mine, Thomas. Tell her . . .
THOMAS	I think she knows!
ROSALEEN	Just before I slept I wished for a handsome prince who would carry me far, far away.
THOMAS	Your wish is granted! Goodbye, young people!

(PRINCE CONAL *and* ROSALEEN *go out hand in hand.*)

So ends my tale. Prince Conal and the little Rosaleen married and lived happily ever after.

(*Applause from the Playwatchers as the Wishing Stone Grove is carried out.*)

END OF FIRST PLAY

 # PLAYWATCHERS

THOMAS	There! Will you take old Thomas, the travelling tinker, to be your Court magician, your majesty?
KING	(*to Bessie*) What do you think, Bessie?
BESSIE	What do I think? Wait and see! That's what I think. Let's have the next one in.
KING	Herald! Bring in the next applicant.
	(HERALD *goes out.*)
	The first one said he could make wishes come true. I wonder what the next one will say?
	(*Enter* HERALD *with* CLEVER JACK.)
HERALD	Bow to the King, Jack! Bow to the King!
KING	This one looks more hopeful. How old are you, Jack?
JACK	Have a guess.
CHAMBERLAIN	Don't answer the King like that.
KING	Stop fussing, Lord Chamberlain. Modern kings have to put up with that kind of thing! (*to Jack*) Your age doesn't matter.
JACK	Why did you ask for it then?
KING	So you think you're a clever fellow, Jack?
JACK	That's right. I can outwit anyone. I can even outwit the Master Demon himself.
ALL WATCHERS	Show us! SHOW US! (*They move to the side.*)
JACK	I'll show you! You'll see me later. (*He goes out.*)

Here begins the story of Clever Jack and the Demons.

Clever Jack and the Demons

Playmakers

BILL
DAN] workmen
DAVE

CLEVER JACK – also called Gipsy Jack

PAT
CONN] friends of Clever Jack
MELL

GOBBLE
GULP
FLIP
FLOP] little demons
PINCH
PUNCH

DANDY DEMON
THE MASTER DEMON
CHASER
CRACKER
Other little demons

Clever Jack and the Demons

Enter BILL, DAN *and* DAVE *carrying a notice and bag of tools. They approach the signpost, which has already been set up.*

BILL   (*reads*) TO DEMON DEN. Well, we're not going down there. We'll nail this notice on the signpost.

DAN   Hold the bottom end, Dave.

DAVE   Give me a hand, Bill. It keeps rolling up.

BILL   Give you a hand! That's what I've been doing all day. I'm the foreman, you know. I shouldn't be doing the work.

DAN   It's all right for some people!

DAVE   It'll be all right for the one who gets that reward. (*reads*) '£100 REWARD.' I wish I could get my hands on that hundred pounds.

BILL   Your hands were made for working, Dave, and don't you forget it. Rewards are a waste of money.

DAN   They're always wasting money at the town hall.

DAVE   Still, they want the thousand pounds back.

BILL   They won't get it back. That thousand pounds is gone, I tell you. GONE! And now they want to waste another hundred pounds.

DAN   Not another hundred pounds, Bill. They would pay the hundred-pound reward out of the money they got back.

DAVE (*reads*) It says:

£100 REWARD

ANY PERSON GIVING INFORMATION LEADING TO THE RECOVERY OF THE THOUSAND POUNDS STOLEN FROM THE TREASURY SHALL RECEIVE A CERTIFICATE OF MERIT AND ONE HUNDRED POUNDS.

Signed TOWN CLERK

BILL There you are! They're giving a hundred-pound **REWARD**.

DAN **TO THE PERSON GIVING INFORMATION LEADING TO THE *RECOVERY* OF THE THOUSAND POUNDS!** But they'd pay the hundred-pound reward out of the thousand pounds.

DAVE Get it?

BILL (*crossly*) I haven't time to stand here arguing. I've got work to do. I'm off! (*He goes out.*)

DAN That's done it!

DAVE I can't think how he got a foreman's job. Here! Hold on a minute. Look who's coming.

(*Enter* CLEVER JACK, PAT, CONN *and* MELL.)

Well, if it isn't Clever Jack and his friends!

DAN Come and read this notice, Jack.

DAVE Everyone says you're a clever fellow, so you can earn yourself some honest money for once!

JACK What do you mean? HONEST MONEY . . . for once?

DAN (*pulling Dave away*) Nothing! Nothing! Come on, Dave. It's four to two! (*They go out quickly.*)

JACK (reads)

$£100$ REWARD

ANY PERSON GIVING INFORMATION LEADING TO
THE RECOVERY OF THE THOUSAND POUNDS STOLEN
FROM THE TREASURY SHALL RECEIVE A
CERTIFICATE OF MERIT AND ONE HUNDRED
POUNDS.

Signed TOWN CLERK

PAT Phew! One hundred pounds!

CONN And a CER. . .TIF. . .I. . .CATE OF
MER. . .IT.

MELL What's that Jack?

JACK It's a handsome card, saying you're a good citizen
and all that.

ALL (laughing) US! Good citizens!

PAT I'd rather have the hundred pounds, myself.

CONN If I had a hundred pounds I'd buy myself a horse
to ride.

MELL I'd buy myself a new suit of fine clothes.

JACK That's just like you! Spending money in your
head BEFORE you have it in your hand. (looking
up at signpost) DEMON DEN! DEMON DEN!
Now . . . I wonder . . . (tapping head) This
robbery could be the work of the demons!

PAT The demons! Do you think it was the demons
who took the money, Jack?

CONN If they did, they can keep it. I wouldn't go near
Demon Den for a million pounds.

MELL What makes you think it's the work of the
demons, Jack?

JACK Ah-ha! (tapping head) I know what I know!

PAT Well, I'm not going to any demons' den to find
out.

31

CONN	Nor me!
MELL	Nor me!
JACK	Then I'll go myself! (*He goes out.*)
PAT	(*shouts*) YOU'RE A FOOL, JACK!
CONN	Jack's not a fool. He's a very clever fellow. Everyone calls him Clever Jack.
MELL	He's a fool to go near Demon Den. They do say there are hundreds and hundreds of little demons in that den.
PAT	There's Dandy Demon too . . . and, worst of all . . . there's the Master Demon himself.
CONN	Don't you think we should go too? Jack's our friend . . .
MELL	Not me! Oh, come on! Let's go back to our camp.

(CONN, PAT *and* MELL *go out. Enter* JACK.)

JACK	(*to the Playwatchers*) They're scared! I'm not! I'm Clever Jack! (*putting signpost over shoulder*) I'll take this away. I'm off to Demon Den. See you later! (*He goes out.*)

Two parts of Demon Den (see p. 64) are carried in by little demons from behind. Chinking of money can be heard.

VOICES OF LITTLE DEMONS	One . . . two . . . three . . . four . . . five! That's a bad one! (*Coin comes over screen.*) Six . . . seven . . . eight . . . nine . . . ten! That's a bad one! (*Coin comes over screen.*)
	(GOBBLE, GULP, FLIP *and* FLOP *come out from behind screen.*)
GOBBLE	Where did they go?
GULP	Over there!
FLIP	No! Over there! (*mad scramble*)

FLOP	I can see one! I can see one! (*He picks one up.*)
GOBBLE	Let go! I want it!
GULP	So do I! (*Fighting begins.*)
FLIP	Give it to me.
FLOP	No! I saw it first! I'm going to keep it.

(*Fighting gets fiercer. Enter* DANDY DEMON.)

DANDY DEMON	Oh no you're not! Wait till Master Demon comes home! I'll tell him about you trying to steal his money.
GOBBLE	We weren't stealing.
GULP	We were throwing the bad ones away.
DANDY DEMON	You were stealing the master's gold coins.
FLIP	This one is bad! Look! (*He bites the coin.*)
FLOP	You try it, Dandy. Go on!
DANDY DEMON	(*biting coin*) NOT BAD! GOOD! Master will boil you all in oil if you steal his coins.

(*Heads of* PINCH *and* PUNCH *appear above screens.*)

PINCH, PUNCH	WHOO-O-O-o-o-o-o-O-O-O-OO!
DANDY DEMON	(*turning round*) What's going on? Bring that money out here.

(*Enter* PINCH *and* PUNCH *with money box.*)

Have you stolen any of master's money?

PINCH	No, Dandy! Not us!
PUNCH	Not us, Dandy! Never! Never! Never!
DANDY DEMON	Start counting those coins all over again. Dandy will watch every one.

(*Enter* JACK.)

JACK	AND SO WILL I!

DANDY DEMON	(*to little demons*) IN! IN! GET IN WITH THE MONEY! IN! IN! IN!
	(*All except Dandy rush into den with the money box and watch from sides and top of screen.*)
	Who are you?
JACK	Some call me Gipsy Jack and some call me Clever Jack.
DANDY DEMON	Clever Jack! Master has talked about you, Jack. Come along in, Jack. Come along in, Clever One.
JACK	I'm not coming IN, thank you very much.
DANDY DEMON	Master wouldn't forgive me if I let you go without inviting you IN. Master will be home before long, so please come IN.
LITTLE DEMONS	(*beckoning*) COME IN! COME IN!
JACK	I'm not coming IN, but that money is coming OUT!
LITTLE DEMONS	WHOO-O-O-o-o-o-o-O-O-OO!
DANDY DEMON	We don't know what you're talking about Jack.
JACK	Oh, yes you do! I'm talking about that thousand pounds your master stole from the town hall treasury.
LITTLE DEMONS	WHOO-O-O-o-o-o-o-O-O-OO!
DANDY DEMON	Master would never forgive me if I talked about STOLEN MONEY, Jack.
JACK	All right then! I'll get my spade and dig a great big pit.
DANDY DEMON	PIT! What pit, Jack?
JACK	The pit for the fire. I'm going to make a fire as big as a mountain. I'm going to build it right up

	against the entrance to your den. AND YOU WON'T BE ABLE TO GET OUT. YOU'LL ROAST ALIVE!
LITTLE DEMONS	WHOO-O-O-o-o-o-o-O-O-OO!
JACK	And serve you right for stealing that thousand pounds from the treasury.
LITTLE DEMONS	WHOO-O-O-o-o-o-o-O-O-OO!
DANDY DEMON	You can't do that.
JACK	Can't I? Ho! Ho! Ho! I can and I WILL, unless you hand over the money box.
DANDY DEMON	We daren't do that, Jack.
JACK	Ah-ha! So you HAVE got it!
DANDY DEMON	Master would bury us in ice and freeze off our fingers, if we gave you the money!
JACK	All right! I'll just go and get my spade while you decide whether you want to roast or freeze.
DANDY DEMON	You CLEVER DEVIL, JACK! (*calls to little demons*) Bring out the money box.

(LITTLE DEMONS *come back in with the money box*.)

	Take it and go!
JACK	Don't worry! I'll be off! (*putting money box in haversack*) Good day to you all! (*He goes out.*)
DANDY DEMON	What shall we do? Master must never know that the money has gone.
FLIP	But Dandy, he'll know!
FLOP	The money's gone!
PINCH	All gone!
PUNCH	Every bit of master's money has gone!

(*Enter* MASTER DEMON.)

MASTER DEMON	(*roars*) GONE! MY MONEY GONE!
	(DANDY DEMON *hides inside the den.*)
	Come here, you little rapscallion! (*taking Flop by ear*)
FLIP	WHOO-O-O!
LITTLE DEMONS	WHOO-O-O-o-o-o-o-O-O-OO!
MASTER DEMON	(*roars*) WHO'S GOT MY MONEY?
DANDY DEMON	(*shakily, looking over screen*) M-m-m-aster!
MASTER DEMON	Dandy! Where's my money?
DANDY DEMON	It's . . . It's . . . It's . . . gone, master.
MASTER DEMON	Come out here, Dandy.
	(*Enter* DANDY, *shaking.*)
	Who's got my money?
DANDY DEMON	A . . . gipsy . . . man. He said his name was . . . Clever Jack.
MASTER DEMON	(*roars*) CLEVER JACK! And who handed it over?
DANDY DEMON	They . . . We . . . They . . . We . . . They!
LITTLE DEMONS	WHOO-O-O-o-o-o-o-O-O-OO!
MASTER DEMON	DAN-DY! (*taking Dandy by ear*)
DANDY DEMON	I did! But master! Jack said he was going to build a fire as big as a mountain, right outside the den. He said that he would roast us all alive.
MASTER DEMON	You'll roast all right! You're a fool, Dandy. You're all fools! How could Clever Jack build a fire out here? He had nothing to build it with, YOU FOOLS!
LITTLE DEMONS	WHOO-O-O-o-o-o-o-O-O-OO!
MASTER DEMON	I'll freeze off your fingers and I'll boil you in oil . . . Dandy!

DANDY DEMON	Yes, master?
MASTER DEMON	Get the freezer on! Boil the oil! (DANDY *goes into the den where he sobs quietly.*) **CHASER! CRACKER!** (*Enter* CHASER *and* CRACKER.)
CHASER, CRACKER	Yes, master?
MASTER DEMON	Chaser! Run after Clever Jack, as fast as you can go, and bring him back here. Cracker! Go with him and crack that whip of yours over Jack's head.
CHASER	I'll chase him, master!
CRACKER	And I'll crack my whip over his head. (*swishing whip in air*)
CHASER, CRACKER	We'll bring him back.
MASTER DEMON	Dandy! Have you got that freezer on? Are you boiling the oil?
LITTLE DEMONS	**WHOO-O-O-o-o-o-o-O-O-OO!**
DANDY DEMON	M-m-m-aster! Clever Jack is very, VERY clever. He'll be too clever for Chaser and Cracker.
MASTER DEMON	Clever Jack is clever all right . . . but what about you, Dandy? What about YOU?
DANDY DEMON	Me, master? Oh. I'm very . . . VERY . . . STUPID!
MASTER DEMON	So what am I going to do about you, Dandy?
DANDY DEMON	You're going to freeze off my fingers and boil me in oil . . . but . . . master . . .
MASTER DEMON	**WELL!**
DANDY DEMON	If you want to get Clever Jack back here, YOU must go after him yourself. Then you can freeze off HIS fingers and boil HIM in oil!

LITTLE DEMONS	(*clapping*) Y-o-u g-o, master! Yo-u go-o-ooo!
MASTER DEMON	ME GO! Not likely! (*scowling at demons*) I know your tricks! I'm staying here.
LITTLE DEMONS	(*clapping*) You stay!
	(DANDY *looks angrily at little demons.*)
GOBBLE	You stay with us in Demon Den, master.
GULP	And then there won't be any trouble.
DANDY DEMON	(*to little demons*) Not for you, maybe. But what about me?
FLIP	Master is going to freeze off your fingers, Dandy.
FLOP	And boil you in oil.
PINCH	Shall we put the freezer on, master?
PUNCH	And boil the oil . . . for Dandy?
DANDY DEMON	No! No! Boil it for Jack! Boil it for Jack!
JACK	(*from off stage*) Stop it! Stop it!
DANDY DEMON	That's Jack! That's Jack's voice!
LITTLE DEMONS	(*running to see*) It's Chaser and Cracker . . . (*They run back.*) AND JACK! (*They run round in circles.*)
MASTER DEMON	(*cuffing all little demons*) Get back inside Demon Den! Go on! Get back inside!
	(*All* LITTLE DEMONS *go inside and peep over screen.* JACK *enters without money box, chased by* CHASER *and* CRACKER.)
CHASER	Here he is, master.
CRACKER	Here's Clever Jack.
MASTER DEMON	Where's my money? Where's my MONEY BOX, Clever Jack?
JACK	MONEY? What money?
MASTER DEMON	(*walking round Jack*) MY MONEY! (*He pats Jack's pocket and looks worried.*) Where is it?

JACK   What are you talking about?

MASTER DEMON   (*angrily*) You know what I'm talking about, Jack. You tricked those stupid demons into giving you my money. WHERE IS IT?

JACK   (*innocently*) Oh that? You must mean that BOX OF MONEY! Your two friends didn't mention the MONEY BOX . . . they just said you wanted to see ME.

MASTER DEMON   (*furiously*) Do you mean that you haven't brought it?

JACK   (*innocently*) No . . . Why should I? Your two friends . . .

MASTER DEMON   (*roars*) Chaser! Cracker! Come here, you rapscallions!

LITTLE DEMONS   WHOO-O-O-o-o-o-o-O-O-OO!

DANDY DEMON   Master! The freezer's on . . . the oil's boiling . . . Let's freeze off their fingers and boil them in oil.

MASTER DEMON   (*in a rage*) I'll boil all three of you . . . I'll boil all three of you . . .

(DANDY *shakes.* CHASER *runs round in circles.* CRACKER *swishes whip frantically.*)

JACK   Stop swishing that whip, Cracker! Anyway, you're supposed to CRACK a whip not just swish it in the air.

CRACKER   Can you do any better, Jack?

JACK   (*grinning*) Much better! I'm Clever Jack, don't forget.

CHASER   Let's see you do it, then.

JACK   If I'm going to crack that whip, you'd all better tie your heads on first.

DANDY DEMON   I told you, master! I told you!

MASTER DEMON	Told me what?
DANDY DEMON	I told you Jack was clever . . . I told you . . .
MASTER DEMON	I haven't seen anything clever about him yet! All right! Let's see you do something clever, Jack.
JACK	Listen, Master Demon! When I crack a whip, I make everyone's head burst open with the noise.
LITTLE DEMONS	WHOO-O-O-o-o-o-o-O-O-OO!
JACK	(*to little demons*) So you'd better all tie your heads on first!

(LITTLE DEMONS, CHASER, CRACKER *and* DANDY *all take off belts and tie them round their heads and under their chins, holding ends in hands.*)

	(*picking up whip*) Now then! Are you all ready?
MASTER DEMON	No! Not yet! Bring me a strong rope.
JACK	What do you want that for?
MASTER DEMON	I've only got one head and I don't want to lose it.
JACK	(*pointing at demons*) They won't get you a rope! They're too busy holding onto their heads.
MASTER DEMON	I MUST have a rope.
JACK	Hang on! I know where there's a rope. I'll get it. (*He rushes out.*)
MASTER DEMON	I MUST have a rope . . . I've got a mighty big head, so I must have a mighty strong rope.
JACK	(*rushing back with long rope*) Here you are! (*He ties rope round Master Demon's head.*) Now . . . what about the ends? Master . . . you can't reach the ends!
MASTER DEMON	Someone must hold the ends! I've only got one head . . .
JACK	AND YOU DON'T WANT TO LOSE IT! I know! I'll call for help! Pat! Conn! Are you there?

40

(PAT *and* CONN *rush in.*)

JACK *cont.*   Hold these rope ends! And just make sure you hold Master Demon's head onto his body when I crack this whip.

PAT, CONN   We will, Jack! We will!

(PAT *and* CONN *stand on either side of Master Demon, each holding one rope end tightly.*)

JACK   (*holding whip in air*) Are you ready? One . . . two . . . three . . . CRACK! (*sound from off stage*)

(PAT *and* CONN *run round Master Demon, binding his arms to his body with the rope.*)

Got you, Master Demon! Got you, at last!

ALL DEMONS   WHOO-O-O-o-o-o-o-O-O-OO!

JACK   (*to demons*) Turn on the freezer! Boil the oil! Dandy! Chaser! Cracker! You can have him! Master Demon is ALL YOURS!

ALL DEMONS   WHOO-O-O-o-o-o-o-O-O-OO! (*They drag Master Demon into Demon Den.*) FREEZE OFF HIS FINGERS! BOIL HIM IN OIL!

JACK   (*walking towards Playwatchers*) I told you I could outwit the Master Demon himself, didn't I?

(MELL *enters, carrying money box.*)

MELL   Jack! Jack! Don't forget the money box!

JACK   (*to his friends*) You can take that back to the town hall and collect the reward. Go on!

(CONN, MELL *and* PAT *go out.* JACK *turns to the Playwatchers again.*)

You didn't think I could do it, did you?

(*Applause from the Playwatchers.*)

END OF SECOND PLAY

JACK (*to King*) So I've shown you that I can outwit anyone, even the Master Demon himself. Now . . . do I get the job, your majesty?

KING I don't know yet. We're very modern here. We're going to vote on it.

JACK Vote on it! You didn't tell me about that.

KING There wasn't time to tell you, because you were in such a hurry to show everyone how clever you are. Now then . . . (*turning to voters*) the first applicant was Thomas the Tinker.

CHAMBERLAIN He showed us how to make wishes come true. That would be very useful, your majesty.

BESSIE You don't need wishes! (*pointing to Chamberlain's group*) You've found good fortunes already, if you ask me. (*Agreement from Bessie's group.*)

KING (*taking no notice of Bessie*) The second applicant was Clever Jack.

CHAMBERLAIN He was such a clever fellow. I'd like to know how to be as clever as that.

BESSIE Clever! You! (*Bessie's group all laugh and point.*)

KING (*taking no notice of Bessie*) We haven't seen the third applicant yet.

BESSIE Then let's have him in.

KING Herald!

HERALD	I'm here, your majesty.
KING	Bring in the third applicant.
	(HERALD *goes out*.)
	I wonder what this one can do.
	(*Enter* HERALD *with the* LITTLE OLD MAN.)
HERALD	Bow to the King . . . I don't know his name, your majesty.
KING	What's your name?
LITTLE OLD MAN	People call me the little old man.
KING	We don't want a little old man! We want a Court magician.
LITTLE OLD MAN	Wait! I have MAGIC power, your majesty.
CHAMBERLAIN	What kind of magic power?
LITTLE OLD MAN	I can give you . . . RICHES!
CHAMBERLAIN	This sounds interesting.
BESSIE	Well, we could certainly do with riches . . . if it's equal shares for all of us!
LITTLE OLD MAN	I can give you . . . GOLD!
ALL	GOLD!
KING	GOLD! PROVE IT!
ALL	Prove it! PROVE IT! (*They move to the side*.)
LITTLE OLD MAN	Very well. I will tell you my story . . .

Here begins the story of Klug and the Golden Goose.

Klug and the Golden Goose

Playmakers

KLUG
FATHER ⎫ Klug's parents
MOTHER ⎭
HERMAN ⎫ Klug's brothers
HANS ⎭
THE LITTLE OLD MAN
LANDLORD of the inn
FREDERICK ⎫ customers
FLOSS ⎭
More people at the inn
FRIZZY ⎫
TIZZY ⎬ landlord's daughters
MOLL ⎭
PARSON ⎫
YOUNG FATHER ⎬ characters at the church
YOUNG MOTHER
NURSE ⎭
KING FRANZ
PRINCESS MIRANDA – his daughter
CHIEF MINISTER

Klug and the Golden Goose

Enter FATHER, MOTHER, HERMAN, HANS *and* KLUG.

FATHER   My back aches! I'm not going to the forest to cut wood today.

MOTHER   But we must have more wood for the fire, husband.

KLUG   I'll go.

FATHER   You, Klug! A fool like you can't use a sharp axe. You might chop your foot off!

HERMAN   Or your leg!

HANS   Or your head!

FATHER   If Klug chopped his head off he wouldn't miss it!

HERMAN   Thick-head!

HANS   Wooden-head!

FATHER   I can't think how I came to have such a stupid son.

MOTHER   Never mind, husband. Herman and Hans are two smart boys. We can be proud of them.

FATHER   Klug is fit for nothing. Just look at him!

MOTHER   Get back inside and wash the dishes, Klug.

(KLUG *goes out.*)

Now . . . who will go and chop some wood for the fire?

HERMAN   What will you give me if I say that I'll go?

MOTHER   If you'll go, I'll give you a big steak and kidney pudding for your dinner.

HERMAN   All right! Give me the pudding and I'll go.

FATHER	(*shouts*) Klug! Bring a big steak and kidney pudding for Herman to take to the forest. You're a good boy, Herman.
MOTHER	You must only cut a little wood, Herman. You mustn't tire yourself. (*calls*) Klug! Hurry up with that pudding.
KLUG	(*from off stage*) Coming! Coming! (*He comes in with the pudding.*)
HERMAN	That looks good! I'll be off! Goodbye thick-head! Goodbye all! (*He goes out.*)
FATHER	What about you Hans? Aren't you going to help your brother?
HANS	What will you give me if I say that I'll go?
MOTHER	If you'll go, I'll give you a juicy rabbit pie for your dinner.
HANS	All right! Give me the pie and I'll go.
FATHER	Klug! Go and fetch a juicy rabbit pie for Hans to take to the forest. You're a good boy, Hans.
	(KLUG *goes out.*)
MOTHER	You must only cut a little wood, Hans. You musn't tire yourself. (*shouts*) Klug! Hurry up with that rabbit pie.
KLUG	(*from off stage*) Coming! Coming! (*He comes in with the pie.*)
HANS	That looks good! I'll be off! Goodbye wooden-head! Goodbye all! (*He goes out.*)
FATHER	Don't just stand there doing nothing while your brothers work in the forest all day. Go into the forest and carry the wood home.
KLUG	(*running towards exit*) I will! I will!
MOTHER	Klug!

KLUG	Yes, mother?
MOTHER	Just see that you don't take any pies or puddings with you. Take a crust of bread for your dinner. Just one!
KLUG	Yes, mother. (*He goes out.*)
FATHER	I can't think how I came to have a son as stupid as Klug.
MOTHER	Don't blame me. He takes after your side of the family. (*Both go out.*)
LITTLE OLD MAN	(*to the Playwatchers*) You've seen how Klug's family treated him! Poor Klug! Just a crust of bread . . . And as you can imagine, the first thing Herman did when he got to the forest was to sit down and eat his dinner! Now . . . Watch! This is where I come in . . .

(*Enter* HERMAN *with axe.*)

HERMAN	What a long way! I can't cut any wood until I've had some of my pudding. Ah! (*beginning to eat*) There's nothing better than a big steak and kidney pudding.
LITTLE OLD MAN	(*walking towards Herman*) And there's nothing I'd like better than a tiny, little piece of steak and kidney pudding.
HERMAN	Well, you won't get any of mine.
LITTLE OLD MAN	I'm very hungry. Couldn't you spare me one tiny bit?
HERMAN	No, I couldn't!
LITTLE OLD MAN	But . . . it's a very big pudding.
HERMAN	And I'm a very big boy, so be off with you!

(LITTLE OLD MAN *moves to side of arena.*)

Oh well! I'd better chop a bit of wood. (*He swings the axe and hits his foot.*) Ouch! OUCH! Help! HELP! I'm hurt! My mother wouldn't want me to work with a bad foot. I'll go back home. (*He limps off, leaving the axe.*)

LITTLE OLD MAN   (*to the Playwatchers*) There goes a mean and selfish boy. And he didn't cut one piece of wood. He thought the axe slipped, didn't he? I wonder how that happened . . .? Ah! Here comes his brother! (*putting finger on lips*)

(*Enter* HANS.)

HANS   There's Herman's axe, but there's no chopped wood. Well, I can't cut any wood after that long walk. I'll have some of my rabbit pie to get my strength back. Ah! (*beginning to eat*) There's nothing better than a juicy rabbit pie.

LITTLE OLD MAN   (*walking towards Hans*) And there's nothing I'd like better than a tiny bit of rabbit pie.

HANS   Well, you won't get any of mine.

LITTLE OLD MAN   I'm very hungry. Couldn't you spare me one tiny bit?

HANS   No, I couldn't!

LITTLE OLD MAN   But . . . it's a very big pie.

HANS   And I'm a very big boy, so be off with you!

(LITTLE OLD MAN *moves to side of arena.*)

I can't think where Herman has gone. Perhaps I'd better chop a bit of wood. (*He swings the axe and hits the side of his head.*) Ouch! OUCH! That was my head! I can't work if I've got a bad head. I think I'd better go home. (*He goes out, holding his head, leaving the axe.*)

LITTLE OLD MAN	(*to the Playwatchers*) There goes another mean and selfish boy. And he didn't cut one piece of wood. He thought his hand slipped, didn't he? I wonder how that happened . . .! Ah! Here comes another one! (*putting finger on lips*)
	(*Enter* KLUG.)
KLUG	(*seeing axe*) This is our axe, so this must be the place. (*calls*) Herman! Hans! Are you there? No brothers! No wood! Now what shall I do?
LITTLE OLD MAN	(*walking towards Klug*) I know what you can do. You can give me a tiny piece of your steak and kidney pudding.
KLUG	But I haven't got a steak and kidney pudding.
LITTLE OLD MAN	All right! Then you can give me a tiny piece of your rabbit pie.
KLUG	But I haven't got a rabbit pie.
LITTLE OLD MAN	What have you got for dinner?
KLUG	Nothing . . . much.
LITTLE OLD MAN	Aha! So you have got something, but you don't want to give any to a poor little old man who is very hungry.
KLUG	No! It isn't that. It's just that I haven't anything good to give you. Look! (*He holds out crust of bread.*)
LITTLE OLD MAN	Is that all you've got, my boy?
KLUG	Yes, just some dry bread. But you are welcome to have some.
LITTLE OLD MAN	Thank you, my boy. You may have only dry bread, but you've got a very kind heart. I think you're worth helping.
KLUG	Do you? No-one else thinks so.

LITTLE OLD MAN	I can see that you haven't got much, so I'm going to give you something worth having.
KLUG	GIVE ME SOMETHING! No-one ever gives me anything.
LITTLE OLD MAN	Go over there and look under the stump of that old tree. There you will find something that will change your whole life. Goodbye! (*He moves aside.*)
KLUG	CHANGE MY WHOLE LIFE! What can it be? I'll have a look . . . OOH! OOH! It's a . . . goose . . . a GOOSE! (*picking up goose*) . . . a goose with feathers of PURE GOLD. Hello, goose! I wonder how you are going to change my whole life? Well, I won't go home. I'll take you with me and seek my fortune. (*He puts the goose inside his jacket and goes out.*)
LITTLE OLD MAN	(*to the Playwatchers*) Now you'll be wondering how that goose could change Klug's life. I'll go on with my story . . . Well, before long he came to an inn.

(*Enter* FREDERICK *and* FLOSS.)

FREDERICK	Ho there, landlord! Ho there!
FLOSS	There's not much going on around here.

(*Enter* LANDLORD.)

LANDLORD	There will be plenty going on later! Girls! Come out here! Frizzy! Tizzy! Moll!

(*Enter* FRIZZY, TIZZY *and* MOLL *with combs, powder puffs, mirrors, etc.*)

FREDERICK	What pretty girls! Who are they?
LANDLORD	These are my three daughters. Yes! They're pretty all right, but they're a bit of a worry.
FLOSS	I can see that! Of course, girls always are a worry. They're much worse than boys.

LANDLORD	Bring out some drinks for our customers, girls. (GIRLS *go out. Enter* KLUG.)
FREDERICK	Here's another customer for you, landlord.
FLOSS	Come over here, boy. Come and join us.
LANDLORD	Not so fast! I don't know about him. What do you want, boy?
KLUG	I'm looking for an inn where I can stay for the night.
LANDLORD	Let me see the colour of your money first.
KLUG	Money! Oh! I forgot about that.
LANDLORD	FORGOT about money! You're not very bright if you think you can have a bed for the night without paying for it.
FREDERICK	What a stupid fellow!
FLOSS	He sounds like a thick-head.
LANDLORD	Where are those girls of mine?
FREDERICK	Doing their hair, I expect.
FLOSS	And powdering their pretty faces.
LANDLORD	(*to Frederick and Floss*) Come along inside. I'll stir them up a bit. (*He goes out.*)
FREDERICK	(*to Klug*) You'd better get some money in your pocket before you come back here, boy.
FLOSS	He's a thick-head! (*Both laugh and follow after the landlord.*)
KLUG	(*taking goose from inside jacket*) Well, little goose! People still call me thick-head and stupid, so you haven't changed that. Never mind . . . we'll sleep over there, under that tree tonight . . . (*holding up goose*) Then tomorrow . . . yes . . . I think you will change my fortune. (*He lies down with the goose under his arm.*)

(*Enter* FRIZZY, TIZZY *and* MOLL.)

FRIZZY   OOoo! Look over there!

TIZZY   It's a young man.

MOLL   And he's carrying a goose with beautiful golden feathers. Come on! Let's go and talk to him.

FRIZZY   Hello, young man! What's your name?

KLUG   Klug.

TIZZY   Hello, Klug. I'm Tizzy . . . she's Frizzy . . . and this one is young Moll.

MOLL   What's that you've got in your arms?

ALL GIRLS   (*giggling*) What is it?

FRIZZY   (*looking at Klug*) OOoo! Isn't he nice?

TIZZY   Do you think he'd like to come with us?

MOLL   I'll ask him. Klug! We're going to the dance tonight. Would you like to come?

KLUG   Mmmm! Yes! I'd like to come, but I shall have to bring my goose.

FRIZZY   You can't do that.

TIZZY   Who ever heard of a goose going to a dance?

KLUG   Well, I can't be parted from my goose. So I can't go with you.

MOLL   Please yourself! Come on girls! Let's go and fetch our handbags. (GIRLS *go out*.)

KLUG   I'm not going to be parted from you, little goose. The little old man said that you would change my whole life, and I do believe you will. I'm tired . . . I'll lie down and get some sleep. (*He lies down under the tree.*)

(*Enter* GIRLS.)

FRIZZY   (*looking in mirror*) I think I look lovely.

TIZZY	All the young men will want to dance with us.
MOLL	There's one who doesn't! Look! Klug is fast asleep under the tree.
FRIZZY	Come on! Let's go!
TIZZY	Have we got everything? Handbags . . . combs . . . powder . . .?
MOLL	Just a minute! I've thought of something. We haven't anything to put in our hair.
FRIZZY	Oh, I wish I had a flower.
TIZZY	Or a jewel.
MOLL	Or . . . I know! I know what we want!
FRIZZY, TIZZY	What?
MOLL	Feathers! Beautiful golden feathers from that goose's tail.
FRIZZY	Do you think Klug would give us one each?
TIZZY	I'll wake him up and ask him.
MOLL	No, don't do that. He might not let us have them. Look! He's fast asleep. Let's just creep up and pull them out of the goose's tail.
FRIZZY	We can't do that Moll.
MOLL	Why not?
TIZZY	It's stealing! Anyway, he might wake up and catch us.
MOLL	Nonsense! We could just say that we were stroking the goose's feathers, couldn't we, Frizz? Go on, Frizz! You go first and then you can get the best feather. (*She pushes Frizzy forward.*)
FRIZZY	(*creeping towards Klug*) I'll get one! I'll get one! Oooo! (*She finds that she can't pull her hand away from the goose's tail.*)

TIZZY	Shh! You'll wake him up, Frizzy.
MOLL	She's trying to get two feathers for herself.
TIZZY	You're mean, Frizzy, you're mean! (*She creeps towards Klug and grabs Frizzy's hand.*) Help! HELP! (*She finds that she can't pull her hand away from Frizzy's.*)
MOLL	(*creeping towards Frizzy*) What about me, then, what about me? Ow! Ow! (*She grabs Frizzy's hand and becomes stuck.*)
LITTLE OLD MAN	(*to the Playwatchers*) Next morning, when Klug woke up, the three girls were still there, all stuck together.
KLUG	That's better! That was a good sleep. Good gracious! (*looking at girls*) Good morning! (*silence*) Can't you speak? Oh well! Don't speak then. I'll be off. (*He gets up.*)
FRIZZY	I'll get one! I'll get one! Oooo! (*repeat*)
TIZZY	You're mean, Frizzy, you're mean! Help! (*repeat*)
MOLL	What about me, then, what about me? Ow! (*repeat*)
KLUG	I can't think what's the matter with these girls!
	(*All go out, girls still repeating their lines. They re-enter on other side of arena, still repeating lines. A young PARSON follows.*)
PARSON	You bad girls! (*All stand still and silent.*) Aren't you ashamed of yourselves, chasing a young man like that? Aren't you? Why don't you answer? Are you too ashamed? You come with me. (*putting hand on Moll's shoulder*) You BAD GIRLS! (*He becomes stuck to Moll.*)
KLUG	I like being chased by these pretty girls! Come on!

(All go out repeating lines, parson saying, 'You bad girls!' They re-enter on other side of arena, still repeating lines. A YOUNG FATHER *follows.)*

YOUNG FATHER   Parson! Parson! Fancy running after those pretty girls! *(All stand still and silent.)* You should be in church christening my baby! *(pulling parson's sleeve)* You'd better go to the church! *(He becomes stuck and repeats, 'You'd better go to the church!')*

(Enter YOUNG MOTHER, *carrying baby.)*

YOUNG MOTHER   What's going on here, husband? Everyone's waiting for the christening to begin. *(pulling husband's arm)* The baby's crying her eyes out! *(She becomes stuck and repeats, 'The baby's crying her eyes out!')*

KLUG   *(laughing)* I am getting popular! Come on!

(All go out repeating their lines.)

FRIZZY   I'll get one! I'll get one! Ooo!

TIZZY   You're mean, Frizzy, you're mean! Help!

MOLL   What about me then, what about me? Ow!

PARSON   You bad girls! You bad girls!

YOUNG FATHER   You'd better go to the church!

YOUNG MOTHER   The baby's crying her eyes out!

(They re-enter, still repeating lines, followed by NURSE.)

NURSE   I'm not surprised that baby's crying her eyes out! What a way to treat a baby! These young mothers have no idea at all! *(putting both hands under baby.)* Come to nursie, baby, come to nursie!' *(She becomes stuck and repeats, 'Come to nursie, baby, come to nursie!')*

KLUG   (*laughing*) One, two, three, four, five, six, seven! All good children go to heaven! Come on!

(*All go out repeating lines.*)

LITTLE OLD MAN   (*to the Playwatchers*) Now it happened that the whole train of them soon arrived outside some palace gates . . . (*turning to watching king*) This was a good old fashioned king. He didn't go in for modern ways . . . Anyway, this king had a problem. His only daughter, the princess, was very serious. She was so serious that no-one had ever seen her give the tiniest smile. The king was in despair!

(*Enter* KING FRANZ, PRINCESS MIRANDA *and* CHIEF MINISTER, *carrying a large book.*)

KING FRANZ   If only you were happy, my dear.

PRINCESS   I do wish you wouldn't keep saying that, father. What is happiness anyway?

KING FRANZ   Look it up, Chief Minister.

MINISTER   But I've looked it up so many times before, your majesty.

KING FRANZ   Then look it up again. You never know, you may find something that would help.

MINISTER   (*spells out*) H-A-P-P-Y . . . happy! Adjective, meaning lucky, fortunate, contented, or, full of pleasure, or, delighted by, or . . . It's no good, your majesty! The meaning of HAPPY stays the same.

PRINCESS   And I shall stay the same until I see something or hear something that really delights me.

KING FRANZ   If only some young man would come along and make Miranda smile – just one little smile – he could have her hand in marriage.

(CHIEF MINISTER *peers out of window.*)

PRINCESS	Then it looks as if I'm going to stay single all my life!
MINISTER	(*excitedly*) There's someone . . . something . . . I can't explain what it is . . . but there's something EXTRAORDINARY coming.

(*Enter* KLUG *and followers.*)

KLUG	One, two, three, four, five, six, seven! All good children go to heaven.
FRIZZY	I'll get one! I'll get one! Ooo!
TIZZY	You're mean, Frizzy, you're mean! Help!
MOLL	What about me, then, what about me? Ow!
PARSON	You bad girls! You bad girls!
YOUNG FATHER	You'd better go to the church!
YOUNG MOTHER	The baby's crying her eyes out!
NURSE	Come to nursie, baby, come to nursie!
PRINCESS	(*jumping up*) Whatever . . .? I'VE NEVER . . .!
KLUG	Hello all! What do you think of my followers? (*He stands still with followers as still as statues, then they move off and start repeating lines again.*)

One, two, three, four, five, six, seven! All good children go to heaven.

PRINCESS	(*calls*) Come back! COME BACK!

(*All come back repeating lines.*)

(*laughing*) Look! LOOK!

(*As princess laughs and calls out 'LOOK', the followers fall apart onto the ground.*)

I've never seen anything so ridiculous! Father! Have you ever seen anything better than this in your whole life?

(*She goes on laughing.*)

KING FRANZ	(*looking at princess*) Never! Never! I've never seen anything better. It's wonderful! In fact, it's a miracle!
MINISTER	(*to Klug*) Young man . . . you're wonderful!
KING FRANZ	What have you to say to him, Miranda?
PRINCESS	Just . . . (*smiling*) . . . that I think he's . . . WONDERFUL!
MINISTER	Your majesty! Do you remember what you said?
KING FRANZ	What did I say?
MINISTER	You said that if only some young man would come along and make Miranda smile . . . just one little smile . . . he could have her hand in marriage.
KING FRANZ	(*clapping hands*) Why, so I did!
PRINCESS	(*clapping hands*) So I won't be staying single all my life . . . if . . . if . . .
KLUG	(*giving goose to little old man and taking princess's hand*) Not IF . . . (*to King*) Just, NAME THE DAY!
ALL	Name the day! Hip . . . hip . . . HOORAY!

(*All go out cheering happily.*)

END OF THIRD PLAY

LITTLE OLD MAN	So you see how my golden goose brought happiness to Klug.
KING	But you said that you had the power to give us gold!
BESSIE	We want gold!
ALL	**WE WANT GOLD!**
CHAMBERLAIN	We don't want a Court magician who just brings happiness.
LITTLE OLD MAN	Ah! But I can give you gold, too. Look! (*holding up golden egg*) My golden goose lays GOLDEN EGGS.
ALL	**GOLDEN EGGS!**
KING	Well, we've got a money problem in this country. We're very short of gold.
BESSIE	Remember! We haven't voted yet.
CHAMBERLAIN	That's right! We must have a proper democratic vote for each candidate.
KING	Very well. Consider your verdict.
	(VOTERS *whisper together.*)
	Show your hands if you wish to vote for the first candidate – the one who showed us the way to make our wishes come true. (*No hands go up.*) So . . . you are not in favour of the first candidate?

ALL	No! No!
KING	Show your hands if you wish to vote for the second candidate – the one who showed us how to outwit the Master Demon. (*No hands go up.*) So . . . you are not in favour of the second candidate?
ALL	No! No!
KING	Show your hands if you wish to vote for the third candidate – the little old man with the golden goose.
ALL	(*waving hands*) Yes! Yes! We want the little old man with the golden goose.
BESSIE	Now we've got wealth and happiness. Three cheers for the King's new magician! Hip, hip . . .
ALL	Hooray!
BESSIE	Hip, hip . . .
ALL	Hooray!
BESSIE	Hip, hip . . .
ALL	Hooray! (*Applause and cheering.*)

Suggestions for the Playmakers

You can make trees for the Wishing Grove like this:
1. Spread out several large sheets of newspaper or wrapping paper on the floor and stick them together edge to edge, until you have a length of about two metres. Paint one side green and allow to dry thoroughly. Paint the other side and allow to dry thoroughly.

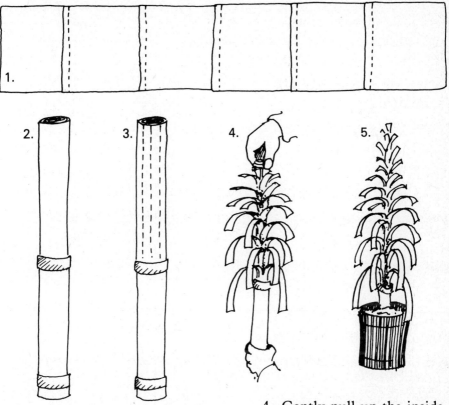

2. Roll the length into a tube and bind sticky tape round the bottom and middle.

3. Make about six cuts from the top of the tube to about half way.

4. Gently pull up the inside of the paper at the top, so that the paper strips hang down like branches.

5. Fix firmly into a flower pot by packing pasted newspaper round the 'trunk'.

If you are a spirit, a bogle or a fairy in 'The Wishing Stone', you can make yourself a paper costume. You will need large sheets of white card, masking tape, green, red and yellow paint, scissors, and a stapler.

1. Cut the card into strips about 5 cm wide and about 70 cm long.

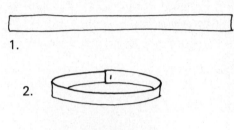

2. Make a 'ring' of card with one strip which will go easily over your head and rest on your shoulders.

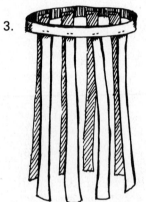

3. Staple the strips onto this ring, leaving gaps for the shoulders.

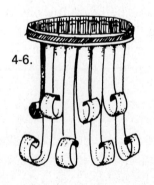

4. Curl each strip by pulling it between your thumb and the blunt side of a pair of scissors.
5. Add shorter strips to the ring and curl them as before.
6. Cover the staples with masking tape.
7. Paint your costume using green paint for spirits, red for bogles and yellow for fairies.

You can make a smaller ring in the same way, to rest on your head, if you are a fairy. Leave a gap at the front for your face.

If you are a demon, you can make yourself a 'sack' costume.

Use a paper or hessian sack, or stitch together two pieces of old material to make a sack shape.

Ask your teacher to mark the places for eye holes and arm slits, whilst the sack is over your head.

Take the sack off. Cut out the eye holes and make slits for the arms.

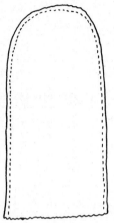

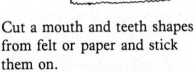

Cut a mouth and teeth shapes from felt or paper and stick them on.

Paint circles round the eye holes and paint on the nostril shapes.

Stitch or stick on lengths of hair made from string, raffia or felt.

Decorate the body of the sack with 'demon' symbols.

Wear black tights underneath the sack costume, and black gloves on your hands.

Coins. Make sure that the coins which are bitten have been throughly cleaned.

You can make the Demon Den like this:

Use two clothes-horses. Attach paper panels to each clothes-horse section. Decorate each panel with 'demon' signs. Hang a 'Demon Den' label between them with string.

You can make a papier mâché goose for Klug:
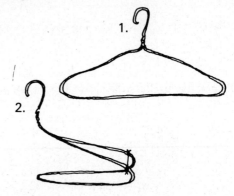
1. Take a metal coat hanger.
2. Bend together the 'wings' and tie them together, Bend the 'neck' to face forward.
3. Fill in the body and head of the bird with crushed newspaper.
4. Paste layers of damp paper over the body and head. Thicken the neck with pasted paper strips bound round the wire.

Paint the goose a golden yellow and stick on crêpe paper feathers.

You can make papier mâché food:
Use foil containers for steak and kidney pudding and rabbit pie. Fill them with crushed paper and paste layers of damp paper over the crushed paper. Build up the layers until you have pudding and pie shapes. Paint them when the paper is dry.

Steak and kidney pudding

Rabbit pie